Eye on AUSTRALIA

EYE ON AUSTRALIA

Photographs by Michael Ruetz

Introduction by Harry Butler

A New York Graphic Society Book · Little, Brown and Company, Boston

First edition

Library of Congress Cataloging-in-Publication Data
Ruetz, Michael.
Eye on Australia.
''A New York Graphic Society Book.''
1. Australia – Description and travel – 1981 –
Views. I. Title.
DU105.2.R84 1987   779.99194   87-3246
ISBN 0-8212-1625-2

Title page: *Farmlands near Munglinup, Western Australia* by Michael Ruetz

Designed by Carl Zahn

New York Graphic Society books are published by
Little, Brown and Company (Inc.).

Printed in Japan by Dai Nippon Printing Company, Ltd.

This book is dedicated to the Australians who go out and challenge the world.

Introduction

Beauty is said to dwell in the eye of the beholder. Every individual makes personal judgements about beauty; some individual judgements, of course, are commonly held and may even become universally accepted as standards within a community or even an entire culture. Unfortunately it is often the case that such perceptions become habitual, unthinking, and thus superficial, however intelligent or sensitive they may originally have been.

This is as true with respect to perceptions of Australia – as a landscape, as a country – as it is for any other subject. Michael Ruetz's unique, unpreconceived vision of this land will come, therefore, as a startling revelation to many.

Few would argue with some basic facts about the fifth continent – the Great South Land:

- It is the smallest continent – until you have to cross it. Then its distances are immense.

- It is the most ancient of lands, so worn down that it appears to retain few natural barriers to movement and expansion; but the waterless sands that burn ochreous in the savage sun of the "Red Centre" are obstacles as formidable as any that exist elsewhere. Australia's is a culture that lives almost entirely around the margins of a burning inland sea.

- Australia's wildlife – its marsupials and monotremes, its gaudy birds and strange reptiles – is always unusual, often unique, as are its natural habitats, covered by trees, plants, and flowers found, almost without exception, nowhere else in the world. Even the smell of the dust, especially after rain, is singularly Australian.

- Australian landscapes are generally monotones of olive, blue-green, or dusty yellow, changing so slowly as to appear endless. There is a hypnotic, almost magical monotony to much of the country – increasingly so as one moves "outback."

These general impressions go unquestioned by the vast majority of Australians – but there consensus often ends. Responses begin to vary as different needs assert themselves. Farmers see the vast stretches of arable land as an enormous granary and produce area, capable of feeding a sizable portion of the world. Miners see an apparently inexhaustible wealth of minerals to supply an eager international community. Conservationists see a wonderland of nature that it is their duty to protect and preserve.

And as valid as all these views are – each in its own way – they are of little significance to Australians of Aboriginal descent, whose very different perceptions of this land are based on forty thousand years or more of undisturbed occupancy. The relationship they established with the land during that time is beyond the comprehension of most white Australians. The ancient myths and everyday lives of the Aboriginal people are intricately and intimately woven into a charter of living that accepts the concept of land as an integral spiritual part of each person.

Today, Aboriginal Australians have adopted – and adapted to – many of the practices of the wider culture, but their personal awareness of and relationship with the land, however shaken, still survive strongly. Indeed, a new awareness of this bond has begun to spread to other Australians and deepen their understanding. With some of their land now safely returned to their traditional keeping, today's Aboriginal people are assuming their proper role as one of the groups that make up the totality of this multicultural country.

Whatever an individual understands of this land, it is a personal response, so in that sense each person's image is valid. For all that, impressions of Australia, especially of Australia as a visual landscape, tend to lack particularity. The habitual and stereotyped always carry a certain vagueness, and even when impressions are precise and clear as to value they are often too fiercely partisan to serve as standards. The conflicting views of loggers and conservationists are a case in point.

There are some images, however, that overwhelm all the members of any culture, and these we tend to deify as the supreme and characterising landmarks of our country. For thousands of years, Uluru, or Ayers Rock, has been such a constant to the people of this continent. The stewardship of Uluru has now been passed back to its original Australian owners. They in turn permit other people to visit this most potent symbol of Australia, recognising its national and international significance. No one really experiences Australia without visiting ''the Rock''; each year hundreds of thousands of people descend upon Central Australia to experience the mystique of this extraordinary monolith. No photographic record of Australia would be complete without its inclusion. It is said with some truth that the colour of Ayers Rock changes with each hour of the day. Countless photographs are taken as everyone strives to capture the Rock's essence for himself; yet even here the end result is too often cliché.

Visitors from other lands and cultures, as a matter of course,

have quite different perceptions from those of locals. Theirs is the stranger's vision, capable of producing insights often barred to those blinded by familiarity. Michael Ruetz, a photographer of German origin, is one such visitor. The harsh sunlight and immense space of Australia, far from overwhelming or alienating him, stimulated him to produce a totally new view of the oldest continent.

Evidence of the sensitivity of Ruetz's perception and of his rare ability to translate that sensitivity into images is found in his published works, notably *Eye on America* and *Scottish Symphony.* These internationally acclaimed volumes are characterised by intense and detailed use of the often sparse light in the subject areas and by a feeling of vast emptiness, unpeopled except by human shadows.

Before coming to Australia Michael Ruetz, as the author, thoroughly researched his new subject. When he arrived he was able to follow a marvellously detailed program and visit a great many of Australia's unique locales and famous landmarks. Following advice from a wide range of local people, he varied this program to take in their special areas, never forgetting his prime purpose – to produce a completely original photographic study, the epitome of unpreconceived observation.

Eye on Australia fulfills his intentions and his purpose. It contains the impressions that were most important to him in his Australian journey. His results show clearly that what this artist has perceived is the timeless land, transformed here and there by the ephemeral workings of man, some of which have taken on a spurious air of permanence. He recognises the destructive transience of man and his works and gently compares this to the apparent permanence of nature.

But Michael Ruetz does not make the mistake of assuming that such natural permanence is static. On the contrary, he captures the immense dynamism of the forces of the earth, and the wholeness of earth systems that is the heritage of all living things.

We often call this wholeness the environment, meaning the sum total of the resources of the earth – physical, natural, and social. The physical and natural elements are relatively steadfast and constant compared to the social – the frenetic, short-lived, seemingly aimless activities of man, which express nonetheless the wonder and beauty of mankind's struggle for excellence and its striving towards tomorrow. Ruetz sees beyond humanity's assumed franchise of the landscape to the deeper reality of natural forces in balance and constancy, but he brings that clarity and depth of perception to his depiction of our towns and cities as well.

Individual choice and individual perception are hallmarks of humanity. Ruetz's interpretation of Australia may not please the traditionalist or the parochial individual who feels that any such interpretation should include all the clichés that are usually regarded as necessary to delineate the "Land Down Under." As I've said, Uluru in glorious colour can be one such cliché, but the images Michael Ruetz has chosen, while unquestionably representing "the Rock," are significantly at variance with those we have come to expect. Even to the most biased local observer, the awareness and sense of place that Ruetz's lens remarkably portrays transcend the lack of dimensionalism so obvious in the efforts of many photographers.

For more than half a century I have lived, travelled, and worked in what I regard, despite a much wider world experience, as the most wonderful country on earth. Indeed, I am charmed and delighted with those non-Australian landscapes and peoples I have encountered. But nowhere else have I found the variety of nature offered so subtly, nowhere else the special blue tinge to the coastal air or the biting smell of the outback, and nowhere else have I found the friendship and kindness of the land and its people as totally as I have in Australia.

Biased opinion? Of course. This is my home, my native and beloved land, and I have spent most of my working life seeking the perpetuation of the components that make it so special for me. My perceptions and understandings have been applied in the main to the often misunderstood and misinterpreted interface between conservation and development, both essential aspects of the continuance of the Australian way of life and the Australian standard of living. The comprehension and concern expressed by a wide range of Australians as a consequence of my work in this area are cause for great personal pleasure and quiet pride. As might be expected, some people have questioned my perceptions, my motives, and my application. This is the traditional Australian way. They have chosen to disagree with my values, and this is as it should be for the widest possible understanding of the complexities of such issues.

I had thought that my perception of native landscapes and the nature of this country was comprehensive, as well as competent and fully aware. But the remarkable presentation of my home put forward by Michael Ruetz has caused me to question those values yet again. Many Australians, on seeing *Eye on Australia,* will realise how limited and shuttered is their vision, and how little they perceive through their rigid views and insular knowledge of the multiple aspects of this great land.

Beauty dwells in the eye of the beholder, and it is often with immense difficulty that we share our subjective views of beauty with other people. Only a gifted few have the ability to share easily, and Ruetz is one of those. The photographs in *Eye on Australia* allow us to enter not only the artist's eye, but also his soul, and so to share his visions. Because so many of us can share these visions, they are entitled to be thought of as constants of beauty, illuminating subtle truths about the land in which we live.

The universal appeal and understanding presented by the images contained in this book transcend the bounds of language, culture, and community. They leave me, as well as others who have seen them, with a marvellous feeling of calm and peace. Ruetz has come as close as anyone can to exposing Australia's essential character.

I hope you, the reader, will enjoy this publication as the personal statement of a newcomer to an ancient land. I hope you will let Michael Ruetz's perceptions and visions offer you a new awareness and understanding of Australia and Australians.

Harry Butler
Perth, 1987

Author's Note

I grew homesick for Australia as soon as the Qantas plane took off from Sydney and I looked down on the city and its unique blend of water and architecture. I had anticipated this nostalgia, but it contrasted sharply with the apprehension I had felt when, two years ago, I first considered the monumental task of photographing Australia.

My trip to Australia was both longer and shorter than I had either planned or foreseen. Longer in that I had never dreamed of driving completely around and right through the entire continent; such a journey had seemed impossible. I managed to accomplish this trip, however, in a shorter span of time than anticipated.

When I think back now about my trip through the enormous vastness of the red part of Australia, I realise that it seemed quite surreal, almost like a journey through outer space, so far away was everything. As we pushed on and on along the endless roads surrounded by endless plains, with unbroken horizons on all sides, I lost my sense of space and time altogether.

In fact, it took me as long to prepare for this work as to actually complete it. It had weighed on my mind for more than a year. Exactly four months before I flew to Sydney, I stopped all photographic work. In a certain way, I had to "charge my batteries." I read as much as I could about Australia – picture books and books by Australian authors – and I prepared myself physically by climbing in the Swiss Alps for six weeks. My "batteries" – now fully loaded – would have to power me throughout the entire journey.

I felt comfortable, almost at home when I landed at Sydney. The chemistry was perfect. The plane touched down at 6:15 A.M., and at 8:00 A.M. I was already working at full tilt. I did not allow myself a cushion of time, but continued pushing myself all through the trip in order to make the most of this opportunity.

Part of the reason why I felt so comfortable in Australia was that this country and all the living beings in it were so good-natured. Australia, like any country, must have its seamier sides, but they were never a part of my personal experience.

What I found in Australia was quite different from what could be garnered from the travel guides, catalogues, picture books, and magazines. The "Aussie" clichés may exist, but I did not look for them. What a relief it was to discover that much of the reality of Australia has been able to escape the ever-tightening grip of the media.

Millions of pictures have been taken (and millions more will be taken) of Uluru (Ayers Rock), the kangaroos, the sleepy-scratchy koalas, the Opera House – we all know by now what they look like. I was determined not to indulge in repetition – or in competition: treating photography as some kind of sporting event; bigger, better, more and even more colour, more exciting, more exotic, etc. I prefer the calm, quiet pictures.

I would classify my large horizontal and double-page spreads as "photographic vedutes," not as "photographic panoramas." I see them as having their roots in the traditions of landscape painting of the last century rather than in the panoramic views of the past few decades.

Panoramas have no specific format or relationship of height to width; they can be of any size. The main point is that they provide an all-encompassing 360-degree view, for which one must, as in nature, turn one's head. The panorama has had a long history in

Michael Ruetz, king wave, at Point Quobba, Western Australia, September 25, 1986

art and was perhaps the first visual "mass medium": one of its greatest advocates was Daguerre himself, whose "Diorama" was popular in Paris and copied abroad. The art of the photographic panorama has a few major proponents; the Czech Josef Sudek, the Swiss Emil Schulthess, the American Art Sinsabaugh, and others were inspired by such painted panoramas. Photographic panoramas are certainly extravagant; they break all barriers, all formats, and extend well beyond the natural measure of the human eye.

The "vedute," as we know it from Piranesi or Canaletto, is a view or "vista" in which the artist looks straight ahead. This is exactly the case with the images in *Eye on Australia*, most of which were taken with a Linhof Technorama camera. These images were composed by placing two views, each with a ratio of 2:3 (height to width), side by side, to give a relationship of 2:6. In reality, we can take in such a view without moving our heads; we see "vedutes" all the time.

Even though these images permit and even invite the observer to let his eyes roam, they are based on the observer's looking straight ahead, not all around or even to the sides. The American writer William Least Heat Moon calls them "two-eyed pictures." Actually, they do correspond – with the 110-degree span – to the view our eyes take in. Each eye deposits a horizontal image in our brain that overlaps the image from the other eye, forming a single, long, horizontal picture.

The break in the middle of this book corresponds to the middle of the face. The two halves of each photograph are composed decentrally – each has a vanishing point – so that nothing can disappear from view. The horizontal orientation and the composition of the photographs correspond to our horizontal mode of seeing. This technique is ideal for photographing the wide terrain and natural wonders found in Australia.

When I try to characterise *Eye on Australia,* I think of it as a symphony of afterimages, part of the palimpsest of the brain that is conjured up long after the trip itself, when I close my eyes and think back to Australia. The further away in time one is, the further back the event of looking at the object, the stronger the afterimage. It is this strength that I wish to give my work: to prepare it for that distant moment when I think back and close my eyes.

A photographic book, just as a work of art, is never the product of only one person. It was all possible because I was lucky enough to be chauffeured by the thoroughly competent Michael Myers of Sydney, to whom I must express here and now my utmost gratitude. Although he had not renewed his driver's licence, he piloted our Ford Fairlane speedily and safely for seven weeks. He managed to stay on the road, avoiding accidents and both live and dead animals. Michael was able to make the trip from Townsville to Uluru (Ayers Rock) – 2599 kilometres – in two days. My sincere thanks go also to my wife, Erica, who made things much easier and speeded up the trip by driving us through Victoria and Tasmania after Michael Myers had gone home. Our daily journey, very often more than five hundred kilometres, almost inevitably ended with the treat of the day: one (or two) bottles of Leeuwin Estate Cabernet Sauvignon 1982, one of the finest wines in the world.

I also wish to extend my thanks to Jan Bradley, Susan Morris-

Yates, and Neil Carlyle of Angus and Robertson, Sydney; to Richard Walsh; to Alan Ward and Vision Graphics, Sydney; to the Bohrnsen family of Lobethal, S.A.; to Ingrid Beck of Hamburg; to H.E. Robin Ashwin and his staff at the Australian Embassy in Bonn; to Lynn Baker, ranger, Uluru National Park; to Michael S. Cullen for working on my manuscript; to Paul Donovan of Ansett Airlines; to Rolf Trümper of Leitz-Wetzlar and the helpful people at Wild-Leitz Sydney; to H.L. Pientka of Linhof München; to Hidehiko Kido and Genichiro Taneoka of Time, Inc., Tokyo; to Ruth von Schnackenburg of Lufthansa Hamburg; and to Terry Reece Hackford, Carl Zahn, and the staff at the New York Graphic Society, Boston. And to all those friendly, helpful, courteous, and kind Australians whose names I never had a chance to learn, and who are the real reason that travelling in Australia – even in the remotest outback – is a pleasant and completely unforgettable experience.

Michael Ruetz
Hamburg, 1987

16

List of Plates